Show Me Your Hands

David L. Derk

Pleasant Word

Pleasant Word (a division of WinePress Publishing, PO Box 428, Enumclaw, WA 98022) functions only as book publisher. As such, the ultimate design, content, editorial accuracy, and views expressed or implied in this work are those of the author.

Unless otherwise designated, all scripture quotations are taken from the King James Version, copyright 1945 by the World Publishing Company.

Revised Standard Version of the Bible, Apocrypha, copyright 1957; The Third and Fourth Books of the Maccabees and Psalm 151, copyright 1977 by the Division of Christian Education of the National Council of the Churches of Christ in the United States of America. Used by permission. All rights reserved.

LL Living Letters

ISBN 13: 978-1-4141-0860-5
ISBN 10: 1-4141-0860-5
Library of Congress Catalog Card Number: 2006908386

My gratitude to Jim and Pat Brocker for their reviewing of my manuscript and their helpful suggestions.

For help with the line drawings, I am indebted to Burne Hogarte and his book DRAWING DYNAMIC HANDS, published by Watson-Guptil Publications/ New York Pittman Publishing/London. (A Division of Billboard Publications)

Dedication

In Memory of My Parents
FRANCIS and GEORGIA DERK

My Father In Law and Mother In Law
CLARENCE and LYNN HUMISTON

My Sister
DORIS IRWIN

Table of Contents

Chapter One

THE HANDS THAT FASHIONED ME

"Thy hands have made me and fashioned me."
—Psalm 119:73

Your Amazing Hand

In the darkness of your mother's womb, a tiny, ivory-colored embryo has entered its fourth week of life. Within that organism, scarcely two inches long, millions of cells are growing at an enormous rate. Soon a pair of "buds" sprout from the side of the neck region and quickly elongate into three separate segments. The outer segment becomes paddle shaped and five lobes soon appear on the edges of that paddle. Muscles, tendons and nerves quickly develop and by the third month of your life miniature fingers begin to move spasmodically. One of the most complex instruments of the entire body has come into being. Your hands have been formed.

Months later when you entered your world you probably clutched the hand of an obstetrician and then the hand of your mother.

I can't think of any feeling in all the world that is as nice as that of a child's hand in mine. It is soft and warm. It speaks of trust saying "Here I am. Shape me. Guide me. Lead me."

A child's hand in yours makes you a symbol of strength and security. A child's hand in yours makes you taller and wiser. A child's hand in yours is your link with life itself. A child's hand in yours is leading you both toward your dreams for tomorrow.

What a marvelous creation is your hand. Your hands will largely determine your life. No other part of the body is so intimately associated with human behavior. With our hands we work, communicate, create and express emotions.

Referring to God as his Creator, the Psalmist wrote, "You made all the delicate, inner parts of my body, and knit them together in my mother's womb. Thank you for making me so wonderfully complex! It is amazing to think about. Your workmanship is marvelous–and how well I know it. You were there while I was being formed in utter seclusion! You saw me before I was born and scheduled each day of my life before I began to breathe" (Psalms 139:13-16 The Living Bible).

What an amazing creation is your hand.

PRAYER

Thank You Lord not only for life but the gift of hands. May I never take such a marvelous gift for granted. Help me to use these hands for Your glory and all of Your creation.

Amen

Chapter Two

THE HANDS THAT BLESSED

"And He took the children in His arms, put His hands on them and blessed them."

—Mark 10:16

Beyond My
Adult World

There is hardly any Scripture that tells of Jesus and children except for an incident mentioned by Mark in his gospel. "And they were bringing children to him, that he might touch them; and the disciples rebuked them. But when Jesus saw it he was indignant, and said to them, 'Let the children come to me, do not hinder them; for to such belongs the kingdom of God. Truly, I say to you, whoever does not receive the kingdom of God like a child shall not enter it.' And he took them in his arms and blessed them, laying his hands upon them" (Mark 10:13-16). This passage in itself emphasizes the importance of children to Jesus, by his recognition of them and giving them his special blessing.

In the midst of conversation dominated by adults we have the sudden intrusion of children.

The disciples saw the children as a distraction to the teaching of Jesus. They were a nuisance and a disturbance to what they felt to be important. Jesus saw what was happening and was displeased. The Scriptures say he was indignant over the way his disciples behaved. If we wish to know what things Jesus cared deeply about, one sure clue would be found in the things that aroused his indignation. Jesus called for the children, took them in his arms and blessed them by laying his hands upon them. Jesus even went so far as to say that "whoever does not receive the kingdom of God like a child shall not enter it."

Jesus was drawing attention to the qualities of child-likeness. He wanted others to see their genuineness, their sense of curiosity, their trust and openness, their dependency and receptivity. Elton Trueblood in "The Heart of a Child" wrote: "God has sent children into the world, not only to replenish it, but to serve also as sacred reminders of something ineffably precious which we are always in danger of losing."

Jesus not only took the children in his arms, he put his hands on them and blessed them. The use of the laying on of hands, to convey a special blessing, goes back to early biblical times. The Levites were set apart for their holy tasks by a special ceremony involving the laying on of hands. (Numbers 8:10) In the New Testament people were set apart for particular religious duties by the laying on of hands.

Jesus saw in children something the adults failed to see so he intruded into their lives and blessed the children who came to him.

PRAYER

Lord help me to see beyond my adult world so I may know the qualities of life that bring your special blessing.

Amen

Chapter Three

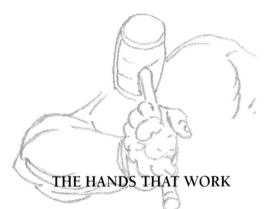

THE HANDS THAT WORK

"…this shows that we are sharing together in the benefits of His body…"

—I Corinthians 10:16 (LL)

Bound Together
As Partners

One of the chief intentions of the Lord's Supper is to experience the partnership among God's people. There is found to be in the participation of Holy Communion a sharing and a fellowship that is more profound than in any other gathering.

The Apostle Paul, in his letter to his Christian friends at Corinth wrote, "When we ask the Lord's blessing upon our drinking from the cup of wine at the Lord's Table, this means, doesn't it, that all who drink it are sharing together the blessing of Christ's blood? And when we break off pieces of the bread from the loaf to eat there together, this shows that we are sharing together in the benefits of his body. No matter how many of us there are, we all eat from the same loaf, showing that we are all parts of the one body of Christ" (I Corinthians 10:16,17 Living Letters).

A wonderful privilege of mine, as a pastor, was to join God's people at the altar of the church and administer the sacraments. As I presented the bread and cup I would notice the hands of those who knelt at the altar.

There were the hands of ushers. These were hands that greeted worshippers with a handshake, offered a worship bulletin or welcomed a new worshipper.

There were hands with a wedding ring reminding us of the importance of love, commitment, and the family.

There were hands that were callous from hard manual labor. Hands that provided not only for a family but the financial needs of the Church and world.

There were ladies' hands that worked in the church kitchen to raise funds for the ministry of the church or knitted mittens for the City Mission or sewed blankets for AIDS babies.

There were the hands of men who lifted chairs and tables for church dinners and times of fellowship or used their skills for church repairs.

There were the hands of Sunday school teachers. Hands that cut and pasted so little ones might learn of the ways of Christ.

There were the hands of an organist whose skill helped us lift our voices in songs of praise.

There were the hands of the elderly that held memories of the past.

There were the hands of youth that guaranteed our future.

The fellowship of the Lord's Table reminds us that we are bound together as co-laborers, as fellow servants and workers.

PRAYER

Thank You Lord for hands that receive the bread and cup at Your Table for they are partners.

Chapter Four

THE HAND THAT BETRAYS

"But behold, the hand of him that betrayeth me is with me on the table."

—Luke 22:21

And There Was Judas

Directed to the second floor guest room of a Jerusalem home, our Lord met with His disciples in an atmosphere of close fellowship. This would be what we have come to refer to as the time of the Lord's Supper. Each had previously had his own personal time with the Lord but now with their varied temperaments and dispositions, they were to share together. There was the impulsive, contradictory, yet lovable Peter. There was Andrew, the man who from the first day that he followed Jesus, had felt a longing to share Him with others. There were two who were named James. James the brother of John and the less prominent James, the son of Alpheus. There was the one whose name means "one whom Jehovah loveth," the disciple John. There was Philip the slow plodder. There was the simple, truthful dreamer named Nathaniel. There was the man known mainly for his faults, doubting Thomas. There was the former tax collector called Matthew. There was the disciple with three names, Judas Lebbaeus Thaddaeus. There was Simon who previously had aligned himself with a sect of hot-Headed patriots called Zelotes. And there was Judas Iscariot.

"And as they did eat, He said, 'Verily I say unto you , that one of you shall betray me.' And they were exceedingly sorrowful, and began every one of them to say unto Him, 'Lord, is it I?' And He answered and said, 'He that dippeth his hand with me in the dish, the same shall betray me......Then Judas, which betrayed Him, answered and said, 'Master, is it I?' He said unto him, 'Thou hast said'" (Matthew 26:21-23,25).

Before Jesus identified his betrayer, each disciple, unsure of himself, asked "Is it I?" There is always the possibility of betraying our Lord and we cannot come to His Table without this disturbing thought facing us. We can even betray Him while outwardly being identified with Him.

As we come to fellowship about the Lord's Supper, let us come in response to His invitation, remembering that this is a time of personal questioning, cleansing, renewing, and discovering that it is God's love which holds us and keeps us faithful.

PRAYER

"We do not presume to come to this Thy table, merciful Lord, trusting in our own righteousness, but in Thy manifold and great mercies. We are not worthy so much as to gather up the crumbs under Thy table. But Thou art the same Lord whose property is always to have mercy. Grant us therefore, gracious Lord, so to partake of this Sacrament of Thy Son Jesus Christ, that we may walk in newness of life, may grow into His likeness, and may evermore dwell in Him, and He in us."

Amen

(From the Ritual of The United Methodist Church)

Chapter Five

THE HANDS THAT CONVINCE

"Except I shall see His hands, the print of the nails, and put my finger into the print of the nails, and thrust my hand into His side, I will not believe."

—John 20:25

Unless I See
His Hands

When Jesus appeared to His disciples on the evening of His resurrection, Thomas was not present. We are not told why but evidently he had difficulty accepting the fact of the resurrection. He must have heard that Jesus had risen and was alive but to accept the word of others was not good enough for him. In reply to the wonderful words that Jesus was alive Thomas said "unless I see in His hands the print of the nails, and place my hand in His side, I will not believe" (John 20:25). He was one who had to see for himself.

The words of Thomas must have reached Jesus, for eight days later, when the disciples met together again, Thomas was present. We read that "Jesus came and stood among them, and said 'Peace be with you.' Then He said to Thomas, 'Put your finger here, and see my hands; and put out your hand, and place it in my side; and do not be faithless, but believing.' Thomas answered Him, 'My Lord and my God'" (John 20:26-28).

Jesus singled out Thomas and met him at the point of his doubt. Neither argument nor scolding was offered but patient understanding. Jesus knew what was in Thomas' mind just as He can read and discern the thoughts in our hearts.

I don't know why faith comes easier to some than others. The Scriptures don't tell us why it took longer for Thomas to believe in the resurrection but if we look at ourselves we might better understand Thomas's problem with faith.

Thomas's lack of faith may have indicated more than just a skeptical mind. Many times we disbelieve in order to protect ourselves. To believe is to risk severe disappointment. Faith involves risk for it's stepping out before we know all the consequences.

Thomas' problem may also have been due to the fact that he had not participated in the community of believers on the evening of the resurrection. Faith always becomes stronger when one is in fellowship with God's people.

It's interesting that the Scriptures do not tell us whether Thomas actually touched the hands of Jesus to feel the imprint of the nails but Thomas responded to the reality of the risen Christ with ecstasy and enthusiasm. This is what is offered to us today–a joyous and exuberant faith in a risen Christ. To Thomas, the resurrection had become more than an accepted belief because of what others said. It was a present, first hand, joyous experience.

PRAYER

Lord, why do I find it so hard to have faith that what You say will come true, especially if it's something as hard to believe as the resurrection? Why can't I just accept the word of others and let it go at that? Why do I have to figure everything out by having everything proven by seeing or feeling?

Help me to be one of those to whom You said, "Blessed are those who have not seen and yet believe." (John 20:30)

Chapter Six

THE HAND THAT OPENS

"Thou openest thine hand, and satisfieth the desire of every living thing."

—Psalm 145:16

Cause for Singing

Psalm 145 has been called the chief of the praise psalms. It was the custom of the ancient Jews to say that "he who could pray this psalm from the heart three times daily was preparing himself best for the praise of the world to come."

We can take heart in witnessing examples of the generous hand of man through the liberality of sharing what he has, but God, unlike the man who limits the recipients of his open-handedness, is the bounteous benefactor of all. "Thou openest thine hand, and satisfieth the desire of every living thing" (Psalm 145:16). To satisfy the innumerable needs of all does not overtax His resources. He has but to open His hand and we are satisfied.

What an encouragement to pray. "He is able to do exceedingly abundantly above all that we ask or think" (Ephesians 3:29). "The same Lord over all is rich unto all that call upon Him" (Romans 10:12).

What an encouragement to live close to the open hand of God. "If ye abide in me, and my words abide in you, ye shall ask what ye will, and it shall be done unto you" (John 15:7). "Whatsoever we ask, we receive of Him, because we keep His commandments, and do those things that are pleasing in His sight" (John 3:22).

What an encouragement in times of trouble. "In the time of their trouble when they cried unto thee, thou didst hear them from heaven" (Nehemiah 9:27).

What an encouragement for all of life. "God is able to make all grace abound toward you; that ye, always having all sufficiency in all things, may abound to every good work: being enriched in everything to all liberality" (II Corinthians 9:8).

Andrew Fuller has written, "God openeth His hand and satisfieth all creation. In what a variety of ways are our wants supplied! The earth is fruitful; the air is full of life; the clouds empty themselves upon the earth; the sun pours forth its genial rays; but the operation of all these second causes is only the opening of His hand! Nay, further: look we to instruments as well as means? Parents feed us in our childhood and supply our youthful wants; ways are opened for our future subsistence; connections are formed, which prove sources of comfort; friends are kind in seasons of extremity; supplies are presented from quarters that we never expected. What are all these but the opening of His hand? If His hand were shut, what a world would this be"

PRAYER

We praise Thee, O God, for Thy bountiful Hand which opens to bless us in nature and grace. Help us to be open-handed always. May our open hands be a sign of Your love and generosity.

Amen

Chapter Seven

THE HAND THAT CARES

"...thou hast strengthened the weak hands."
—Job 4:3

Out of My Need You Came

Milton and Lillian Barnes grew the most beautiful dahlias I had ever seen. That is one reason I purposely took the route that went by their home and garden whenever I took my daily walk. They chose to grow flowers on a corner lot which could have brought a good price in their affluent neighborhood.

One evening I received a telephone call that Lillian had suddenly and unexpectedly died of a heart attack. Milton was devastated. The following weeks, as I passed the corner lot, I noticed the garden was being neglected. It mirrored the heart of the one who had lost his partner in growing dahlias.

Milton continued working part-time in the greenhouse of the local florist and shared with me a letter he had received from a fellow worker.

Dear Milton:

There is no doubt in my mind that everything is going to seem meaningless to you, for a while. Having had someone so close who shared your thoughts, plans and confidences for so many years that you felt you were one, is indeed a difficult obstacle to overcome.

You must learn to become single again. Instead of "we" you become "me". It's best to face it head-on and not pretend that when tomorrow comes that it really didn't happen. In time, you will be able to do this and each day will be easier for you to deal with. I never thought at one time that I could ever be "me" again. It's been over one year now and although I felt I was on the edge of falling–I hung on, kept busy, did anything, went everywhere that anyone suggested. That is how I came to work for Forbach's–never having worked during my married life–they took a chance on me–and I took a chance on them. I have to admit it's been a challenge; but it made me pull myself together. I found I had an inner supply of strength because I had to have it. Many people find that supply when they are under a strain. You will find it too. Time does help so "Hang in there."

There are many things to be coped with: your home, your family, your friends. You just find that you do the necessary things and the doing of it helps you.

Sincerely,
Marjorie Nicholson

With the help of God and friends Milton once again began to grow the most beautiful dahlias in the world.

PRAYER

Thank You Heavenly Father for those who take pen in hand and strengthen our hands so they may once again grow dahlias.

Amen

Chapter Eight

THE HAND THAT LEADS

"Even there shall Thy hand lead me, and Thy right hand shall hold me."

—Psalm 139:10

A Ride on a Goatskin Raft

It all happened when the Communists were on their long march from South China to the North. They were already in Kansu Northwest China and heading our way. Foreign governments had warned their nationals to evacuate before it was too late so we traveled to Lanchow, the capital of Kansu, where we met other missionaries and their families.

There were two routes open to escape the Communists. The shortest route was by trucks but they had to leave before we would be able to go. They left without us and were later captured by the communists, robbed and all the people killed. The other means of escape was to travel down the Yellow River by goatskin rafts. This method of transportation had been used by the Chinese for hundreds of years in order to transport their wool, hides and other goods in a convenient and inexpensive manner.

At that particular time business had been disrupted so the rafters were glad for work. Goatskins were also apt to deteriorate with time so they were ready to travel. Goats were carefully chosen, killed and the skin preserved by skinning it over the head. The hide was tanned; they were then turned inside out so the hair was inside; the legs and neck were sewn tightly so the entire goat skin could be inflated. There were thirty of us so we planned for two large rafts. Each raft consisted of about twenty-five goat skins tied to a square framework of small logs, the framework being held together by hemp ropes. The raft rode high out of the water and because of its lightness proved to be more buoyant and maneuverable for the river rapids. Six skilled raftsmen managed each raft with three in front and three at the rear. Each raftsman steered the raft with a long stout wooden oar. For most of the way the river would be wide so the men were fully able to shoot the rapids and manage the whirlpools.

For shelter and sleeping quarters, small semi-circular shelters were made from green willow boughs tied together and fastened by rope to the raft. Mats of split bamboo were placed over this framework and then topped by oil cloth. Bamboo mats made up the floor where we would sleep. Food was cooked on a charcoal fire. Supplies were replenished enroute at specific stops familiar to the raftsmen. This would be a journey of twenty-eight days.

At the close of each day the rafts were tied to stakes that had been driven into the ground at shore and the raftsmen slept over the ropes so they would be awakened in case the raft left its mooring.

There came a night I will never forget. Supper had been good and family devotions had fed our souls. The stars were shining. My two sisters and I had gone to bed. Everything was calm and peaceful. Then it happened. There was a strange rush of water, so much so that the rafts began straining at their mooring until the stakes were pulled out of the ground and the raft began drifting out into the rapid river current. The quickened current began twisting the raft causing some of the skins to burst. My sisters and I awoke thinking we would have to follow the previous plans our parents had told us to follow in case of any emergency. My mother and I would stay together and try to hold on to a floating log or goat skin, my two sisters would be with dad. After what seemed an eternity the raft suddenly came to a halt when it became stuck on a raised portion of land in the middle of the river. When daylight came we found that we had become stuck just before one of the most hazardous parts of the river.

After repairing damages to our rafts and taking a day for rest we continued our journey through Mongolia and the Ordos River and finally to Paotingfu where we went by train to Peking.

PRAYER

Thank You Lord that there isn't a place on earth where you can't lead us or hold us safe.

Chapter Nine

THE HAND THAT SETS US FREE

"…for freedom Christ has set us free…"

—Galatians 5:1 (RSV)

Finding Freedom

I will never know how the little sparrow entered my home. Perhaps he came through a door ajar or window left open. I only know that he was here and he taught me some lessons about life.

Frantically he flew from room to room seeking to find the freedom of his home outdoors. I tried to guide him to an open door yet he failed to understand my intent and continued darting here and there until he finally came to rest, clinging to a curtain. Reaching to take him in my hand I found no resistance for all his efforts to find freedom had utterly exhausted him. Fearing his escape I held him firmly, until his throbbing heart became normal, then taking him outdoors, with open hand I lifted him to the sky. He now was free once again.

Now that my feathered friend has found his freedom, I have been thinking of him and asking myself some questions. Was he the one who frequently visited the feeder outside my kitchen window? Never having been confined to a hand does he now understand his freedom?

I also think of the lessons taught me by the little sparrow.

The desire for freedom is built into creation. The caged lion pacing back and forth, the fish released from the hand of a fisherman, the bird that sings in its cage and the person held in the grip of a habit, each yearns for his or her freedom.

Life's circumstances can hold us hostage. Fears can keep us captive. Those are the times when we need to remind ourselves that God can bring us out of our bondage. I can view God in a way that leads me to think of Him primarily as loving and kind, for that is easy to see. When life is comfortable and all is going well, I can easily assume that God is in His heaven and all is right with the world. There may come, however, times when I need the hand of God that frees me from the harsh realities that hold their grip on me—times when I can experience the unconditional grace and forgiveness of God and live a life of freedom and fulfillment.

PRAYER

Thank You Lord for having said that You know about every sparrow and that I am more valuable than many sparrows. Thank You for reaching out and taking me in Your hands, especially when I fly in all directions, not knowing where I am, heart throbbing with fear. Thank You for holding me until it's safe to set me free again.

Amen

Chapter Ten

THE HAND THAT GIVES

"…you shall open your hand…to the needy and the poor,…"

—Deuteronomy 15:11

Tea Leaves

Returning from a furlough in the United States it had now been three weeks since we left Hong Kong on our way to a mission station in Northwest China.

We were in an area that had been devastated by war, famine and disease. Stopping at an inn, in a small village, we found lodging on the second floor where we could have three rooms. The center room we used for our luggage, the other two rooms for relaxation and sleeping. Supper would be served later in the day so the inn keeper brought us hot water to wash up before tea would be served. After tea had been served he took the tea cups and put them on a table in the center room, then closed the door for our privacy. Following a brief rest I entered the center room to check our luggage and noticed a small Chinese girl had already entered the room. It was difficult to really know her age because of her physical condition but I guessed her to be approximately eight years of age. A flimsy garment reached only to her knees, emphasizing her thin legs. Her eyes showed the fear of my discovery of her. She was eating the tea leaves that had been left in the bottom of the cups. We later learned from the inn keeper that she had been left an orphan. Other families had very little to share with her so whatever she could find to eat helped her survive. That evening and the following morning, just prior to our departure, we made certain she had something to eat.

Compared to the rest of the world, few of us in the United States have ever experienced hunger or known others who were hungry. When we do hear of the huge problem of starvation elsewhere it seems so enormous that we become complacent or paralyzed by inaction. It is so easy to feel that we cannot do much about such a large problem. When we really come to grips with the unequal apportionments of even such human necessities as food and clothing, the Christian steward wants to do something. There are agencies that try to meet the needs of people but private efforts are needed. We must personally work to alleviate hunger and assist the poor to become self-supporting. When we are tempted to feel helpless about the hunger and poverty afflicting millions we must remember that each individual is a brother or sister.

PRAYER

Help me Lord to get my eyes in focus so I can see the needs of those who are far away as well as those who are close by. Make me aware of those who need such necessities as clothes and food or just a word of encouragement. Help me to recognize their needs before they are too shy to ask.

Amen

Chapter Eleven

THE HAND THAT UNDERSTANDS

"And He came and took her by the hand…"
—Mark 1:31

Reaching Out
with Your Heart

The Scriptures mention several occasions when Jesus took a person's hand.

"Now Simon's mother-in-law lay sick with a fever, and immediately they told him of her. And he came and took her by the hand and lifted her up, and the fever left her" (Mark 1:30, 31).

"But taking her by the hand, he called, saying, 'Child, arise.' And her spirit returned, and she got up at once" (Luke 8:54,55).

"And they came to Bethsaida. And some people brought to him a blind man, and begged him to touch him. And he took the blind man by the hand, and led him out of the village" (Mark 8:22, 23).

"But Jesus took him by the hand and lifted him up, and he arose" (Mark 9:27).

"He took (her, him) by the hand!" When Jesus healed Peter's mother-in-law of a fever, he took her by the hand. When he restored the daughter of Jairus to her father and mother, he took her by the hand. When he healed the blind man, he took him by the hand. When he made well the boy who was possessed of a demon, he took him by the hand.

Jesus understood the fears and hopes of others. He saw their problems and difficulties. He thought with their thoughts and felt with their feelings. He cared deeply about others who needed His touch so He put His feelings into action. He took the hands of others.

It is the hands that often make the difference between intending and doing.

When you take a person by the hand you are saying:

> "Right now, you are the most important
> person in my life.
> I care about the way you feel.
> I want to be a part of your life.
> I am with you. We are in this together.
> I know what you are going through and
> I'll be by your side.
> Together we can make it.
> I understand.
> Let me lead you."

To take someone by the hand means making the first move. It is surrendering your indifference and identifying with another. It means putting good intentions into action. It means reaching out with your heart.

Prayer

Lord help me to be sensitive to the needs of others. Give me an understanding heart as I take the hands of others.

Amen

Chapter Twelve

THE HANDS THAT PRAY

"Lord, I have called daily upon thee, I have stretched out my hands unto thee."
—Psalm 88:9

Pray with Expectancy

Nowhere in the Scriptures are we directed to fold our hands in prayer. Prayer is always associated with hands that are "lifted up," "spread toward heaven," or hands that are "stretched out to God." I like the picture of "outstretched hands" because they speak of a sense of expectancy. Outstretched hands are ready to receive. They await the gift with anticipation.

Do you pray with expectancy? Do you expect God to listen? Do you expect prayer to make a difference? Evidently the psalmist expected prayer would make a difference in his life for he wrote, "Lord, I have called daily upon Thee, I have stretched out my hands unto Thee" (Psalms 88:9).

The psalmist also wrote in Psalm 143, "Hear my prayer, O Lord; give ear to my supplication! In

Thy faithfulness answer me, in Thy righteousness" (vs.1)! He then continues, "I remember the days of old, I meditate on all Thou hast done; I muse on what Thy hands have wrought. I stretch out my hands to Thee; my soul thirsts for Thee like a parched land" (verse 5,6).

A time had come in the life of the psalmist when he felt he had nearly come to the end of his expectations that God would ever intervene in his life so he stretched out his hands to God. He would try the way of prayer and put his trust in the faithfulness of God. He remembered that in the history of his people there were countless illustrations of how God had answered prayer but what was happening now was personal. There were discouraging circumstances surrounding him. There were choices being made for him that were beyond his control, yet out of all this there came a calm, determined expectancy as he stretched out his hands to God. Hands that had hung so helplessly at his side were now lifted in prayer. Hands that had been useless for lifting were now lifted up in power and purpose. Through prayer he could even touch the strong hand of God. He now expected that God in His mercy would respond. He stretched out his hands to God.

PRAYER

There are times Lord when I only wish to speak to you without really expecting something from You. Sometimes I only want to thank You for life and blessings. Sometimes

I just want to "get something off my chest."
There are, however, times when I pray with
expectancy. Expecting an answer, I lift my
hands to You.

Teach me how to pray–expectantly.
Amen

Chapter Thirteen

THE HANDS THAT CREATE

"And the vessel he was making of clay was
spoiled in the potter's hand, and he reworked
it into another vessel, as it seemed good to the
potter to do."

—Jeremiah 18:4

Unseen Possibilities

It was only a blob of wet clay—a mass without form or beauty…possessing no apparent ability to evolve into a vessel of value and usefulness. The clay had to submit itself to the skilled hands of the potter and the potter's wheel. Only then would it be on its way to becoming a thing of beauty and value.

As Jeremiah watched the deft fingers of the potter begin to form a vessel, something went wrong. The vessel was spoiled. In his mind the potter had an image he wanted to create but the intended vessel did not become a reality. He knew that the potter and the clay were both involved in the same creative process. The potter knew from experience the intricacies and frustrations of creating a vessel. Lack of success was not new to him. He could not always complete his first desire. Failure of the moment, however, did not mean failure was final. The clay still held possibilities. So he made it over again into another vessel.

In God's hands the unseen possibilities of our life can become real. God can see the deeper, inner meaning that is part of each of us. He sees beyond the surface. There is more to us than what we see in the mirror. There is a part of us not always visible.

The potter did not discard the piece of clay. Neither does God discard us. He does not give up on us but with persistent patience seeks to refashion us. God sees possibilities that others may fail to detect. No life is beyond God's remaking. None of us are beyond the restoring hand of God. He can take us in His hands and fashion us anew.

Ask Him to do that for you today.

PRAYER

Lord, You and I know that deep down inside me I want to love You enough to be willing to be like clay in Your hands but sometimes I am more like hard cement than soft clay.

I know You love me. You have shown me in so many different ways that You care about me. Still, I seem to have some reservations when I ask you to mold me and make me like You.

Try again. I'll probably protest and complain but together we know what's happening… more Christ-likeness is developing.

Amen

Chapter Fourteen

THE HAND THAT WEARS A RING

"...the father said to his servants, 'Bring forth the best robe and put it on him and put a ring on his hand and shoes on his feet.' "

—Luke 15:22

When We Return

Luke gives us the story that has come to be known as The Parable of the Prodigal Son. Two sons received their inheritance from their father. The younger son took the money and left home. He quickly wasted his money to the extent that he became destitute. Finally realizing that life on any terms would be better than what he was experiencing he decided to return to his father.

Luke writes: "So he returned home to his father. And while he was still a long distance away, his father saw him coming, and was filled with loving pity and ran and embraced him and kissed him. His son said to him, 'Father, I have sinned against heaven and you, and am not worthy of being called your son.' But his father said to the slaves, 'Quick! Bring the finest robe in the house and put it on him.

And a jeweled ring for his finger; and shoes! And kill the calf we have in the fattening pen. We must celebrate with a feast, for this son of mine was dead and has returned to life. He was lost and is found.' So the party began" (Luke 15:20-24).

The father had been watching and hoping for his son's return. Each passing day ended with disappointment and less of a chance for the mending of their broken relationship. One day, however, as he looked down the path, he saw his son. He recognized him in his rags. His son could not disguise his step. Every feature of his son had been remembered and wept over. His son was returning

The father did not know if his son had changed or was repentant of his actions. He didn't know if he had learned anything from those wasted years. He only knew that he was coming home.

What a welcome he had. There were no words of sharp reproach. There were no requests to be met for acceptance. There was the fullness of a father's love and understanding. The finest robe in the house replaced his rags. Shoes were fitted to feet that had no shoes. A ring was put on his finger, the ring being the sign that his father meant his words of welcome. He was not only welcomed in grand style but he was now restored to a place of dignity and honor. What a beautiful picture of a broken relationship being restored.

Lloyd Ogilvie in his book *A Life Full of Surprises* uses the phrase "the liberating power of affirmation." The father's embrace, his kisses, the robe, the shoes and the ring were tokens of acceptance and affirmation. We need such times in our lives and we need to show such times to others. We need times of reconciliation. We need to free others from condemnation and judgment and give them reassurance and validation. Reconciliation can come when one's life is recognized and appreciated.

PRAYER

Thank You Heavenly Father for this picture of reconciliation. Help me to be your instrument for reconciliation. Allow me to take the first step of embracing another so reconciliation can begin.

Amen

Chapter Fifteen

THE HAND THAT WAS RESTORED

"...and his hand was restored whole as the other"

—Mark 3:5b

Confronted by Our Limitations

Once again it was the Sabbath, the best day of the week for begging and from experience the man with the withered hand knew the synagogue to be the best place for begging.

The Scriptures do not tell us why his hand was deformed. Maybe he had been born that way or had a disease that caused his hand to be misshapen. He may have accidently severed the nerves and tendons of his hand so he could no longer use his hand. Tradition tells us that he had been a mason by trade and represents him as beseeching Christ to heal him in order that he no longer be compelled to beg for his daily bread. His condition was such that he was an object of pity. His hand was useless, with all power gone as completely as if death had seized it. There appeared no alternative to what fate had dealt him. He must have been painfully conscious of his shrunken, shriveled hand as it hung helplessly at his side.

The beggar went unnoticed to the habitual worshipper but today there was one person who did notice him. In fact, the Scriptures say that Jesus was deeply disturbed by the indifference to human need shown by others. The one who did notice him however was the one who could help him. "Stretch forth thy hand" he said. There was no manipulation or harsh command, just a simple directive and in doing as he was bid his hand was restored whole as the other. In his obedience he found his limitations turned to capabilities.

Today there are those who can't seem to put forth their hand to give to the poor or minister to others. This paralysis has its source in the selfishness which lives without love, in pride which excludes all others, in the greed which hoards all in its grasp, in the refusal to alter old habits, in the distrust to venture in faith. Hands that have become complacent in their lack of action.

We need hands that are eager to produce good in the world about us, hands that are energetic and not afraid to work, hands that are willing to be used and eager to be a positive force.

Prayer

Our Heavenly Father, so often we have failed to stretch forth hands that have become withered. Let Thy Holy Spirit direct and control us so the limitations we place upon ourselves may become our possibilities...possibilities to serve Thee and others.

Amen

CPSIA information can be obtained at www.ICGtesting.com
Printed in the USA
BVOW042100230412

288387BV00001B/5/A